I Just Want To Quit But I Can't

Pastor Dr. J.W.T. Spies

Table of Contents

Unless otherwise indicated, all scripture quotations are taken from the King James Version of the Bible

A View About The Author

Pastor Dr. J.W.T. Spies, a distinguished native of Chicago, has dedicated over 50 years to the ministry of God's Word. He presently holds the position of Senior Pastor and Visionary Leader at Praise Tabernacle Ministry Church in Jackson, MS.

Dr. Spies is married to Dr. T. Nichole Spies, and together they are the parents of four children: Christopher, Raheem, Savannah, and Faith. Their family also includes two bonus daughters, Britney and Dulce, and four grandchildren, Carter, Camdyn, Maximiliano, and Nylah.

Dr. Spies is committed to the church's mission of evangelizing the lost, uplifting believers, and demonstrating love to fellow Christians, as prescribed by scripture.

Pastor Spies has pursued extensive theological education through esteemed institutions, including the

Chicago Bible Institute in Chicago, Illinois; Mt. Hermon Bible Institute in Fort Myers, Florida; Texas Bible Institute in Baytown, Texas; Oklahoma Bible Institute in Muskogee, Oklahoma; and Newburgh Theological Seminary in Newburgh, Indiana, where he earned his Doctoral Degree in Divinity.

In addition to his academic achievements, Dr. Spies is a distinguished musician and recording artist. He established his own recording choir, "Power of Praise," in 1998.

Recognized as one of the most gifted and anointed preachers of his generation, Dr. Spies excels in both traditional and contemporary preaching and gospel music. His diverse skills and dedication position him uniquely to impact lives and advance the Kingdom of God through his ministry.

Dedication

I would like to dedicate this book first to my late father and mother Reverend James S.C. and Caruther Spies who inspired me to be all that I could be in God.

To my wife Evangelist Dr. T. Nichole Spies, my children Chris, Raheem, Savannah, Faith, Britney, and Dulce. To my G-Babies, Carter, Camdyn, Maximiliano, and Nylah who in a special way helped inspire me in writing this book. (I want to thank you all for the love and support down through the years). To all of my family members who have kept me lifted up in their daily prayers. To my brothers George, the late Deacon Vincent. To my late sister and brother Harriett, and Vincent, sisters Eileen, Netter, and Lisa, and all of my In-laws.

Acknowledgement

My sincere thanks to all of those who have had either a direct or indirect part of my ministry. To the late Reverend James O. Conner and his lovely wife Pastor Ernestine Conner along with the St. Rome Full Gospel Church for cultivating me in my young stages of ministry. To Pastor Reverend Dr. Mack McCullom, I thank you for the intense Boot Camp Training of Ministry. To Dr. William Glover who loaded me with creativeness and vision. To my Pastor Reverend Dr. Donald L. Parson, thank you for all of his motivation, inspiration, and impartation of sharing with me how to take the limits off of God, and for teaching me almost everything that I know about ministry and its structure. To my cousin who has encourage me and prayed over the years Debra (Clay) Mines, and to my special prayer partner for years Pastor Woodard (Woody) Williams.

Special Thanks

To my church family where I Pastor, Praise Tabernacle Ministry Church. To Apostle Michael and Denise Gaulden who has inspired me down through the years (It's your time). To my late God brothers Derrick Patrick, Lansing Lee, and to my God brother Jerome Baker.

To Dr. R.K. Moore who has taken me under his wings, to tutored me, guide me, and lead me as the Spirit of God has directed him as a Shepherd in my life. I thank you for all of the impartation that you have given me as a Pastor.

To Dr. Donal L. Parson, Dr. T. Nichole Spies, Dr. Danny R. Hollins, and Dr. Jonathan T. Phillips Jr., I wish to extend my heartfelt gratitude to each of you for taking the time from your demanding schedules to contribute the Forewords and Afterwords. Your support means more to me than words can convey, and I am deeply appreciative of your efforts.

Foreword

Pastor J.W.T. Spies, in his first book, invites us to address issues that remain unaddressed in most places where people in ministry gather to have unedited expressions with each other. Often our true emotional experiences are rarely shared.

Pastor Spies challenges us to address our hidden frustrations, and unexpressed disappointments with doing ministry. His provocative title invites the honest among us to shout, me too!

This book will quietly remind you that the journey to this moment was filled with seasons like the ones experienced by the characters who expose their humanity in each chapter.

We all owe the author a debt of gratitude for his reminders of the times we've felt like "Running but knew that we could not hide.

Spies' honesty and transparency is refreshing as he shares his recollections of an emotional rollercoaster while appearing steadfast, and full of faith, doing daily ministry.

He was being challenged by the paradox, of the prosperity of the unrighteous and the struggles of those in pursuit of the footsteps of Christ. The results of his observations concluded "It just ain't Fair! Who among us have not felt the same?

This book will be a literary tonic, for those ready to Quit! Dr. Spies' book will remind you of your lowest moments, but it will inspire you to rise from the Church Steps, because we can't quit!

Reading this book should help those who are about to surrender to the wounds, of ministry warfare, to get to Him quickly. It is in his presence that we are reminded that we have a mission assignment. So, we never quit, we can't quit, we don't go awol, we complete the mission.

Dr. Spies presents the human perspective, but ultimately leads us to the conclusion with a dynamic spiritual manifesto on why we cannot quit. This is a must read

for every believer.

Dr. Donald L. Parson
Logos Baptist Assembly
Chicago, IL

Foreword

In the quiet, vulnerable hours of the night, when the demand of ministry weighs most heavily, many pastors find themselves on the edge of giving up. Dr. J.W.T. Spies is no stranger to this struggle. His journey, as chronicled in this powerful and deeply personal book, mirrors the anguish, frustration, and spiritual wrestling found in Psalm 73. Like Asaph, the psalmist, Dr. Spies found himself asking a piercing question: *Is it worth it?* The countless sacrifices, the betrayals by those who should be allies, and the deep wounds inflicted by the very people he was called to Shepherd seemed to overshadow the joy of serving. It is a question many in ministry face, but few voice.

Psalm 73 tells the story of a man who struggled with envy and doubt, questioning why the wicked seemed to prosper while the righteous suffered. Dr. Spies echoes this same tension, exposing the raw and often unspoken pain of a pastor's heart. Yet, just as Asaph found clarity when he entered the sanctuary of God and saw beyond the immediate, so too did Dr. Spies. In the midst of his deepest despair, he chose to continue the course, clinging to the call God placed on his life, knowing that God's purposes extend far beyond the present challenges.

This book is a testament to resilience, grace, and the power of God's presence in the midst of adversity. It is an honest exploration of the hardships faced by those in ministry, but more importantly, it is a declaration that *quitting is not an option.* Dr. Spies invites you to walk with him through the valley, to wrestle with your own doubts and fears, and ultimately to find the strength to persevere.

Whether you are a pastor, a ministry leader, or

someone simply seeking encouragement in your faith

journey, this book will provide you with both the validation

of your pain and the tools to overcome it. Dr. Spies does not

offer a sugar-coated narrative; instead, he shares the raw

truth of ministry life while pointing you back to the eternal

hope we have in Christ.

By the end of this journey, you will be reminded that

God is faithful, even in the darkest moments, and that the

call He has placed on your life is worth every trial. As Psalm

73 concludes, "But as for me, it is good to be near God; I

have made the Sovereign Lord my refuge; I will tell of all

your deeds." Let this be your anthem as you continue to

serve faithfully, knowing that God is with you every step of

the way.

Dr. J.W.T. Spies has not only lived this truth, but he has also emerged from his own valley stronger and more resolved than ever to fulfill the call of God. This book is his gift to you—an invitation to join him in choosing faith over despair, hope over surrender, and perseverance over quitting. As a licensed therapist, I find the contents of this book to be profoundly healing for every person wrestling with the temptation to surrender when adversity strikes from all sides.

Dr. T. Nichole Spies

Dr. T. Nicole Spies, LMFT, MS, NCC, DMin
H.O.P.E Family Counseling

Introduction

Late one evening, after a particularly demanding and thought-provoking day of ministry, I found myself reflecting on whether the effort was truly worthwhile. I questioned whether ministry was worth enduring the numerous challenges, including the emotional and spiritual roller coaster, and the pain and sorrow that accompany it.

I pondered whether I should tolerate the betrayal from those who profess love and consider themselves my Christian brothers and sisters, even as they seemed to inflict pain at every opportunity. Despite their outward displays of friendship, their actions felt like a constant assault. At that moment, I came to understand the Old Adage, "With friends like these, who needs enemies?"

Many of you have experienced similar emotional turmoil and have faced the temptation to give up, with some of you having already done so. However, I am here to offer encouragement: you are not alone, and there are spiritual solutions to these challenges. By the end of this book, I hope you will find ample guidance and scripture to reaffirm your resolve and remind you that quitting is not an option.

Chapter One
You Can Run But You Can't Hide
Jonah

Ninety seven percent of my messages is about my life and what God has done for me in my life, and as I looked over the life of this biblical character, I found some very similar traits of this man's life in the life of many of those of today's society who call themselves Christians as well as non-Christians.

As we investigate the life of this Hebrew boy, and then stop and take inventory of ourselves in the mirror, if we truly be honest with ourselves, we will notice that there have been times in our life when we have run parallel with the lifestyle of this man named Jonah.

In the active city of Nineveh, during the chaos of everyday living, there lived a man named Jonah. He was no ordinary man; he was a prophet, chosen by God, to deliver a message from God by the divine orders of God, this message was to be a message of warning and wisdom to the people of Nineveh. But there was an issue, a problem and a dilemma here, because Jonah was burdened by a feeling that gnawed at his soul and spirit, Jonah didn't want to do it, Jonah had no desire to go to Nineveh, in fact, Jonah had the desire to quit.

One day as Jonah strolled through the busy streets of Israel, he heard a voice that stirred, shifted, and filled his heart with dismay, and apprehension. The voice of God spoke to him in a divine way charging him to voyage to the city of Nineveh and give a message of repentance.

Jonah's voice echoed with unwillingness as he pleaded with the Lord saying, surely, God, you must mean somewhere else. Nineveh? You don't understand, God. Those people down in Nineveh are idol worshipers. You know those people in Nineveh are hard-headed, and they won't listen. God, send me anywhere else but Nineveh. In speaking His words carried the weight of fear and uncertainty, a desperate attempt to evade the frightening task laid before him.

This ancient story of Old, unfolds in the book of Jonah chapter one by saying "(*Now the word of the Lord came unto Jonah*", *or and the Lord spoke to, or Jonah and God had a conversation, and he said to Jonah, Jonah arise, and go to Nineveh*). However, knowing the situation, the circumstances, and the problems of Nineveh there was the desire to flee, and say I just want to quit.

Devastated by fear and the uncertainties, Jonah is now faced with a choice: he could adhere to the call of God or just abort the assignment. His decision was made, Jonah decided to disregard the voice of God divine orders, and he boarded a ship bound for Tarshish, expecting to escape his divine mission and find comfort in the ambiguity of the sea.

Obviously, Jonah had not heeded the saying of the people of old, because my grandmother used to say that a hard head would make a soft attitude. May I tell you that there are always consequences to our actions when we don't follow the mandates of God's divine instructions.

The narrative of his thinking didn't turn out like he thought it would, because fate had other plans for Jonah. As the ship navigated across the ocean, a mighty storm prevailed upon them. Waves crashed against the hull; the winds howled like a ruthless beast. Panic clutched the sailors as they realized their doom was forthcoming.

Now watch this because this is very important, whenever we don't do what God has told us to do and whenever we go in a different direction than what we have been instructed; we will have to pay a price.

In verse three it says, "(*But Jonah rose up to flee unto Tarshish from the presence of the Lord,* (it's always a danger when we leave the presence of the Lord) *and went down to Joppa; and he found a ship going to Tarshish: so, he paid the fare thereof, and went down into it, to go with them unto Tarshish from the presence of the Lord.*"

Secondly, when we go in a different direction then where God sends us, we will always have some troubles, heartaches, crisis, alright some storms. If we are not careful, we just might in up being arrested by the winds and waves of verse four as Jonah did. (vs 4) *"But the Lord sent out a great wind into the sea, and there was a mighty tempest in the sea, so that the ship was like to broken."*

Third, when we don't obey the Lord, we will include others in our problems that we about to encounter with God.

Verses five and six give us a description. *"Then the mariners were afraid, and cried every man unto his god, and cast forth the wares that were in the ship into the sea, to lighten it of them. But Jonah was gone down into the sides of the ship; and he lay, and was asleep. So, the shipmaster came to him, and said unto him, What meanest thou, O sleeper? arise, call upon thy God, if so be that God will think upon us, that we perish not."*

In other words, whenever we go against what God has assigned us to do, we will have to go farther then we want to go, and we'll have to pay more than we want to pay, and we will have to stay longer than we want to stay.

Jonah jumps on this ship and as soon as the ship set sail God sent his H.B.I'S out, that's heaven bureau of investigators out to arrest the ship, in other words God spoke to nature and said bring the billows in, he spoke to the elements and said winds I want you to toss them to and fro. He told the lightning to start clapping and the thunder to start roaring. He told the clouds to cover up the sun so that there be no light. I heard that somebody said the captain of the ship said, I have seen many storms in my life, but I have never seen one like this one before.

So, I heard that he commanded the other sailor to get rid of the heavy load so that the ship might be lighter so that they would not capsize. But even after they had empty everything off the ship that might weigh it down, I heard that the captain said, n'all boys it's something else wrong here.

During some of the struggles that I've encountered in my life, I had a conversation with my older brother (George) who informed me that this struggle that you are in is not yours alone, but you are involving other members of the family in your mess, which didn't make sense to me at the time because my vision was clouded.

When we attempt to distance ourselves from God, our actions impact those around us. For instance, if we seek refuge at our parents' home, we draw our entire family into the situation. Similarly, if we head to the nearest airport, we involve everyone present there.

Jonah's presence endangered everyone aboard the ship, prompting the captain to advise all passengers to call out to their respective gods, as the vessel was on the verge of disaster. At that moment, a sailor inquired about the individual below deck, and it was decided that someone should go down and awaken him.

I can hear them asking him, how can you sleep in a time like this, don't you know that we are about to die, are not you scared about what is going on? So, the bible says that they begin to cast lots, and the lot fell on Jonah. And I heard Jonah say, there is no need to worry I know what the problem is, the problem is me.

Isn't it remarkable how individuals often recognize that they are the cause of their difficulties—essentially the reason God is unsettling their situation—and yet remain silent? They might experience external turmoil, such as disruptions or threats, without addressing the underlying issues.

Someone might question, "Pastor, I've been wondering why I haven't seen progress or why everything I attempt seems to fail." The answer could be that there is someone within your circle or group who is distancing themselves from God. To move forward, it may be necessary to address and resolve the influence of that person in your life.

Jonah acknowledged his identity and informed them that he was the cause of their troubles, suggesting that throwing him overboard would resolve their issues. However, Jonah was unaware that God, having foreseen the situation, had prepared a great fish to ensure his safety. Consequently, when Jonah was cast into the sea, the fish was already positioned to receive him.

In the midst of his disobedience, the chaos of the sea arrested Jonah. Jonah found himself cast into the sea, swallowed whole by a great fish. Trapped in the darkness of its belly, he wrestled with his doubts and fears, consumed by the weight of his decision to flee from his destiny, and quit the mission assigned to his hands.

In the solitude of the belly of this beast, Jonah cried out to the Lord begging for forgiveness and redemption. In his moment of despair, he discovered the true purpose of his journey, and that was to bring hope and salvation to the people of Nineveh. With a newfound resolve, Jonah vowed to fulfill his divine mission, no matter the cost.

Just like Jonah, I have had some days when I didn't feel like going to Nineveh, my Nineveh was not located in Assyria, my Nineveh was in the churches that I pastored. My Nineveh was with those that didn't want to hear what thus said the Lord. My Nineveh was dealing with deacons that felt they knew the vision better than the Under-Shepard. My Nineveh was fighting against by-laws that superseded the Word of God. My Nineveh was fighting against the people that I was supposed to be fighting alongside of. My Nineveh was dealing with a church that put the provision for my family in jeopardy. Nineveh often had me saying that I Just Want To Quit.

It is often that the weight of church made it easier to want to stay at home then to follow the directions of God. This is how the enemy tricks us off the path that has been paved for us.

But it was when I was swallowed up by the big fish that I realized that I needed to repent and get back to what God had instructed me to do. In this story something miraculous happened, it was like Jonah made the fish sick, because the great fish released Jonah from its belly, and he emerged from the depths of the sea, reborn and renewed. With a heart full of purpose, he set out on his journey to Nineveh, ready to face whatever challenges lay ahead.

It was in the life of Jonah that we were able to see the Power of Redemption. As Jonah entered the city gates of Nineveh, he delivered the message of repentance to the people. To his amazement, they listened and heeded his words, turning away from their wicked ways and seeking forgiveness. In that moment, Jonah realized the true power of redemption — that even the darkest of storms can lead to the brightest of dawns.

It was in the life of Jonah where there was an Embracing of Destiny. With his mission complete, Jonah found peace in knowing that he had fulfilled his divine purpose. No longer burdened by the desire to quit, he embraced his destiny with open arms, ready to face whatever challenges the future may hold.

Although there was an embrace of destiny, in the life of Jonah we will Find Hope in the Storms. At the end of Jonah journey, we are taught a powerful lesson — that even in our darkest moments of doubt and despair, there is always hope, to be found. No matter how strong the storm may rage or how deep the rivers may run, God can give us the strength to overcome any obstacle to fulfill our true purpose in life.

I am here to emphasize that while we may attempt to escape, we cannot evade the presence of God. We might seek refuge in the mountains, but He will find us there. We might retreat to the valleys, but He will be there as well.

In essence, no matter where we seek solace—whether it be in substances, the embrace of a lover, or other forms of distraction—God will locate us. David himself attested to this truth, declaring that even if he made his bed in hell, God would find him there. He noted that there is no place where we can truly hide, as every attempt to conceal ourselves is futile.

Therefore, the safest and most secure refuge we can seek is in the arms of the Lord, who is always waiting for us. We must not abandon our path; we are called to persist in listening to and following God's guidance, remaining

steadfast in our commitment to His directives.

Chapter Two

Why Won't Trouble Leave Me Alone

Luke 6:22-23

22 Blessed are ye, when men shall hate you, and when they shall separate you from their company, and shall reproach you, and cast out your name as evil, for the Son of man's sake. 23 Rejoice ye in that day, and leap for joy: for, behold, your reward is great in heaven: for in the like manner did their fathers unto the prophets.

For many years, I have desired to undertake a thorough investigation into this physical disorder. This inconvenient element, this confused emotion, this transitive verb that has been photographed and etched in my mind, as trouble. For quite some time now, I've been wondering and pondering why is that trouble seems to intensify and lift its heads in my life so much.

I must confess that at the pinnacle, the apex the zenith, and the combination of them all, has lately been a puzzling question, that why it in this modern day I still filled bombarded, overwhelmed, and literally saturated with what seems to always look like and feel like there is a crisis in my life.

I have frequently questioned why the gray clouds of anguish, torment, agony, and suffering persistently hoover and linger in various aspects of my life. It appears these troubles stubbornly remain in the places where I seek solace and peace.

To be honest I have often baptized my thoughts in curiosity of how wonderful it would be if my present existence never made contact, or a connection, with any pain, setbacks, or disappointments.

I have often wondered, as some of you might, whether there will ever be a time in my life when I can experience a period of complete tranquility—when I might enjoy a few weeks free from trouble, with no problems or crises working against me.

I fantasize about serenity and tranquility of just a little quietness, let me just say it like I feel it, I just wonder can a brother just have some peace in the valley, and a piece of mind.

I know that this all sounds good, but when I finally came back to myself, back to the common reality, reality reminded me that life on this planet will not allow me to submit to such a utopia, a paradise or dreamland. In fact, reality has shouted back to me, boy you just need to wake up.

Reality gave me some insight, reality gave me a rude awakening and a shaking, as Job said, *"that man that is born of a woman is of a few days, and those days are filled with trouble."*

I don't know about you, but it just seems to look like

this human man, and this life, is just a magnet for drawing troubles and problems. So, being conscience of these facts, the question that hangs in front of my mind is what now. I say that I Want To Quit, But I Can't.

What now should we do, when trouble comes down upon us, what should we do when we are pressed on every side, what should we do when we are persecuted, struck down, and forsaken? I asked the question, what should our behavior be?

Should we make the attempt to run, flee, and try to escape out of desperation? Should we become a fugitive from trouble? Or should we just give up, give in, and tap-out.

I have good news for you when we are going through difficult times. We should never overlook or dismiss *Psalms 34:19 which say's "Many are the afflictions of the righteous,* (but here is your shout) *But the LORD delivers him out of them all."*

My brothers and my sisters we should never forget about *John 16:33,* which says *"In the world we will have some tribulation; (here is your second shout) but be of good cheer, because I have overcome the world."*

Please don't forget about *2ⁿᵈ Timothy 3:12,* which say's *"And all who desire to live godly in Christ Jesus, will suffer some persecution."* Whatever you do don't discard John 15:20 that tells us to remember the word that I said to you, *"that a servant is not greater than his master. And if they persecuted Me, they will also persecute you."*

So, I say to you my brothers and sisters, we must not ever get sidetracked by the certainties or uncertainties of trouble. We should not ever get to the point where we as Christians think that we are exempt from trouble.

I must acknowledge that, while I am not fond of trouble, it often seems to find its way into my life. Although my flesh resists adversity, my spirit embraces it, as my spirit is aligned with God. God is aware that challenges will arise with the intent to test, destabilize, and harm me. Nevertheless, I have confidence that God possesses the power to deliver me from these trials.

Let me see if I can clarify this matter by conducting a thorough, spiritual examination of trouble, and place it under what I call a spiritual, microscopic evaluation to gain deeper insight. First, we must consider how to address the myriad manifestations of trouble, given that throughout history, no group or individual has successfully eradicated it. Neither has any faction been able to eliminate trouble, nor has any extremist been able to intimidate it, and politicians have been equally ineffective in influencing it. Trouble seems to persist as an enduring presence. Therefore, as Christians, it is essential to understand how we should navigate and respond to the challenges it presents.

Well, as I began investigating the neighborhood of Hebrews the other day, and while I was scrolling my way through the biblical landscape of 1st Peter to get some understanding on this matter, in between time, it was right there. In between the 13th chapter of Hebrews, and between the 5th chapter of 1st Peter, I seen it.

It was compacted, nestled, condensed right there between Hebrews and 1st Peter that the optic nerve of the transparent lens of my eyeball accidentally bumped into this masterpiece of Godly literature, right in front of me there it was the Epistle of James chapter one verses one through three.

In this scriptural landmark I finally found out what we should do in the time of crisis. James shared with me what to do when trouble attacks us without a moment's notice, it's right here in the book of James. Now I am familiar with this James, for he is the same James who was once a skeptic of Jesus but later became a devoted servant. This is the same James who was believed to be the half biological brother of Jesus. This same James that was the bishop at the church in Jerusalem, and now he is emphatically saying to count it all joy when we fall into divers' temptation.

I said whatttttt!!!!! Count it all joy? Yes, because James understood what the men and women of God were going through. It was from this type of agony that James was propelled to write upon his pad of this epistle.

After his greeting in verse one, He says my brethren, which renders references to the body of Christ. He said my brethren count it all joy when you fall into diver temptations.

And some of you all are already looking funny, because can you imagine after going through all of the hell that you have gone through, and someone comes up to you, telling you to count it all joy while we are going through.

So, I really got excited when I started reading Luke 6 and 22, because this is a shocking passage to the world, for Jesus switches the world's values completely around. He rejects entirely the materialism things of the world, and he warns us that one day judgment is coming.

Verse 22 teaches us, that *"blessed are the persecuted, those who are persecuted for Jesus' sake."* The persecuted are those who endure suffering for Christ. Jesus spelled it out what He meant by Blessed. He means Blessed are those who are being hated, ostracized, reproached, and having one's name spoken against.

The Lord gives us this adjective that we are Blessed. It doesn't matter that people are talking about you, just know that you are Blessed. It doesn't matter that people don't want to be your friend, just know that you are Blessed. So, what they don't want to have tea with you, you ought to have it by now, just know that you are Blessed.

The Lord here wanted us to know what type of attitude a person is to have while being persecuted. The person is to "rejoice" and "leap for joy." The Lord wants us dancing and shouting, smiling and cheesing, when the enemy lifts their hands against you.

I can hear someone saying, I heard you, but Pastor how is this possible for me to smile, laugh, and rejoice when I'm dealing with all of this? I'll tell you how it is possible by keeping our eyes on the reward, and not the problem, because when we are focused on the problem it helps us to focus on quitting. When we concentrate on the problem, it helps us focus on quitting. When our attention is distracted by the issues in our life and not the promises of the Lord we will think about quitting. We need to focus on the promises and not the problem, because God has been solving problems long before we began having them. He is a problem solver.

So, the writer says rejoice. Let's look at the word rejoice. The Greek word for Rejoice is χαίρω which means to be in a state of happiness and well-being, *rejoice, be glad.* "Rejoice and leap for joy; for when you rejoice and leap with joy, the bible says, *"behold, your reward is great in heaven."* When you are going through, and you rejoice it confuses the enemy, he questions how is it that I'm hitting them with my best shot, and they are still happy, still praising, they are still shouting and giving glory to God. He says, "Rejoice and leap for joy."

Here it is. We as Believers are forewarned, that we will suffer some persecution. Believers suffer persecution because we are not of this world. We are called out of the world. We are in the world, but they are not of the world.

We are separated from the behaviors of the world; it doesn't mean we won't mess up, but it's because we don't want to stay the way we are, and because of that, the world reacts against us.

Put Word to it Pastor, well, John 15:19 says. *If ye were of the world, the world would love his own: but because ye are not of the world, but I have chosen you out of the world, therefore the world hateth you "*. Believers suffer persecution because they strip away the world's robe of sin. We must do our best to live and demonstrate a life of righteousness. Believers suffer persecution because the world is deceived. But there is a promise to the persecuted.

The Bible says that our reward is great in heaven. The promise is that the persecuted will receive a great reward. As a saved person no matter what we are going through we ought to be able to find a way to tell the Lord thank you. So, I need to tell somebody:

Never get upset when trouble comes knocking at your door. Never get upset when trouble arrives in your zip code.

Never get upset when you must go down to the lowest valley, because we must know that trouble doesn't last always.

I'm reminded of a story that was told about a carpenter who had hired a young man to help him to restore his old homestead, but on the first day he had a rough day on the job. On the first day he lost his keys to his truck that made him miss an hour of work. When he finally made it to work, the chain saw that he brought to work refused to crank. The old man that hired this young man heard about his problems, he decided to pick up the young man and invited him to his home for dinner. While riding to the old man's home, they rode in silence.

Upon arriving at the home, he invited the young man in to meet his family. As they walked toward the front door, the farmer paused at a small tree, touching the tips of the branches with both hands. When he opened the door, he underwent an amazing transformation. His face had a smile on it, and he hugged his two small children and gave his wife a kiss. After dinner, he walked the young boy to the car, and as they passed the tree, the young man curiosity got the best of him. He asked him about what he had seen him do earlier. He asked why is it that you rubbed the tree on your way into the house? The old man responded, "Oh, that's my trouble tree." "I know I can't help having troubles on the job, and in my life, but one thing's for sure, troubles don't belong in the house with my wife and the children. So, I just hang them on the tree every night when I get home, and I leave it there." Brothers and Sisters, may I tell you that we have a tree that we can hang our troubles on.

He is the tree of life.
He is my burden bearer.
He is my way out of no way.
He is my bread for my breakfast.
He is my heavy load sharer.

So, even though trouble won't leave me alone, even though there are days that I am pressed on every side. I realize that I can't quit because I have a leaning post that will hold me in the time of trouble.

Chapter Three

It Just Ain't Fair

Psalms 73:2-5
² But as for me, my feet were almost gone; my steps had well nigh slipped. ³ For I was envious at the foolish, when I saw the prosperity of the wicked. ⁴ For there are no bands in their death: but their strength is firm. ⁵ They are not in trouble as other men; neither are they plagued like other men.

On this occasion, Asaph the psalmist took the time to carefully observe his surroundings, noting the actions of both the wicked and the righteous. He made a point of assessing the behavior of the unrighteous alongside that of the righteous.

Asaph made a clear effort to view the ways of the wicked, compared to the ways of the righteous. He took inventory of what the unrighteous were doing, and what the righteous were doing. It is obvious that Asaph seen the contrast of how the wicked were progressing, and how the righteous were not.

When we read the text, we see that Asaph had devoted time to observing the Godly, and the ungodly, Asaph has seen a great difference in how the righteous faired, opposed to how the unrighteous is fairing. He noticed how the righteous were constantly struggling, while the wicked seem to be always prospering. This episode deeply troubles and distresses Asaph, nearly overwhelming him. My brothers and sisters, this troubled the psalmist to see the wicked prospering and flourishing while the righteous continual to be in poverty and in their struggles. And I think I ought to tell you that Asaph had some serious problems, even with God.

To sum it all up, for those of you who are following all the rules, and to those of you who are staying prayed up.

It appears that you are fasting and following all of the guidelines of the Word of God. And when you see what the wicked is doing, and you're not doing, it makes you want to say to yourself it just ain't fair.

We might wonder why it seems that the wicked, the unrighteous, the evil, sinful, immoral, unlawful, vicious, vile, and those of darkness seem to be thriving while we struggle to get by. It just doesn't seem fair. I wanted to address this topic because there may be some individuals who are grappling with some issues similar to those experienced by Asaph.

And the reason some may feel this way is because you have endeavored to cross all of the T's, you have made sure that you have dotted all of the I's, but it seems as though still you see nothing but struggle while the ungodly continual to prosper. And it makes you want to scream, "It just ain't fair!".

It feels unjust that despite my dedication to prayer, fasting, and supplication, I continue to face challenges while others who do not engage in these practices appear to thrive. It seems particularly inequitable that my children are struggling, whereas others seem to receive undue advantages. I wish someone would acknowledge that this situation is profoundly unfair.

Allow me to quickly acknowledge that while our subject may not be grammatically perfect, I believe this phrasing effectively conveys the sentiments we are aiming to express. I understand that I could have simply stated, "It just isn't fair," but that expression may lack the gravity we're aiming for. Therefore, if you would indulge me and allow me to phrase it like I feel it, to better capture the sentiment we seek. "It just ain't fair!"

My brothers and sisters, the text reveals a profound dilemma and significant anxieties on the part of Asaph. While time constraints prevent me from elaborating on every nuance of these concerns, allow me to emphasize that the psalmist was deeply affected by issues strikingly akin to those that many of us contend with today.

You see, Asaph had decided to live for God, he had committed himself to walk, and to talk in a Godly fashion, he had endeavored to live his life that it would be pleasing to the almighty God. But his plight, as is the plight of many believers, was one of stress and strain, and one of a tremendous struggle, and his problem was made even greater when he looked at the unrighteous having no struggles, or problems at all.

The burden on the man of God was so immense that he expressed it by stating his feet nearly slipped, indicating he was on the verge of backsliding into worldly ways. In simpler terms, he almost gave up. This may seem trivial, but for those of us who have faced extreme financial pressure— where bills such as electricity, gas, rent, food, water, and other necessities are overwhelming—it can lead one to contemplate desperate measures. It's a situation where one might think, if only I could momentarily escape my struggles to regain stability. The feeling of wanting just one more chance to recover, or seeking a brief respite to alleviate the pressure, is a profound challenge.

I, too, have experienced the weight of contemplating how much simpler it might be to revert to my former ways. I've pondered what it would be like to return to a state of chemical imbalance.

When observing those who seemingly thrive, such as individuals flaunting wealth and luxury while I struggle with an unreliable vehicle, it's disheartening. The disparity can provoke a sense of injustice. When faced with the distress of a child suffering from hunger or discomfort due to a lack of resources, while witnessing others seemingly prosper and display their earnings, the feeling of unfairness becomes overwhelming. The financial strain, coupled with the inability to seek assistance due to past debts and ongoing struggles, only intensifies this perception.

The pressures of life can lead one to contemplate drastic measures. Pressure, after all, can cause water to flow, pipes to burst, and can lead to severe health issues such as strokes and heart attacks. I must confess that I have been in a similar situation as Asaph, where I felt on the brink of despair and have privately voiced the sentiment that it is indeed unfair. It seems particularly inequitable that despite my earnest efforts to live righteously, those who disregard or are indifferent to spiritual values often attain everything they desire.

Yes, I know how Asaph felt. I can feel you Asaph. Asaph, I understand that the struggle is real, and I believe I have identified the root cause of Asaph's predicament. Are you interested in hearing my perspective? It seems that Asaph's primary issue stemmed from an excessive focus on the wicked. He devoted too much of his valuable time and energy to dwelling on their negative influence, rather than channeling that focus towards a more positive and uplifting endeavors.

I believe we face a similar issue today. We often invest excessively time focusing on troublemakers rather than addressing the needs of those who are genuinely hurting. We tend to spend more energy on those who stir up discord than on individuals experiencing true spiritual struggles. Similarly, we frequently expend significant effort pursuing and addressing gossip, rather than dedicating our time to engaging with the teachings of the Gospel and seeking personal spiritual growth. Yes, He devoted to much time observing and watching what the ungodly was accomplishing. May I tell you that when we consistently focus on negative or detrimental influences, it can and will have a deep and contrary impact on us.

If I had the opportunity to speak with Asaph, I would advise him to shift his focus away from the wicked and turn his attention to the Lord. I would encourage him to look to the hills from where his help comes. By focusing on the Lord, he would find protection, joy, and an unspeakable peace—qualities that come to those whose minds are steadfastly set on Him.

Now I don't want you all to get this wrong Asaph was a man of God. Asaph loved the Lord, but how many of you know that you can be a child of God and still be focusing on the wrong things. Asaph observed and questioned why the wicked seem to prosper while the righteous suffer. In seeking my personal understanding, I asked God why it appears that the wicked are blessed while we are not. The first insight He provided was that what appears to be greener grass on the other side of the fence might be artificial turf. Furthermore, the cost of maintaining that facade— symbolized by a higher water bill—implies that they will ultimately pay for what they perceive as prosperity. Secondly, he said that everyone isn't ready for a blessing, everybody can't handle a blessing right now.

The third thing that he said to me which had the most impact, is that you haven't seen, or you can't see the end result of those who are prospering in an ungodly fashion. Those who think that they have gotten away, they haven't gotten away at all. Because the Old Adage says that they might get by, but surely, they won't get away. He said that my feet almost slipped. And if most of us were to be honest with ourselves, some of us are some almost slippers, we have some almost slippers in the pulpit, we have some almost slippers in the choirs stands, we have some almost slippers on the deacon ministry, and if we go on and to tell the whole truth some of us has went beyond almost slipping, and just stepped on into it. Yes, there have been times when we all have slipped.

However, here's a reassuring fact: and that is, if you have nearly fallen or have completely fallen, God will not abandon you. There are many here who can attest to having come close to slipping or having fallen entirely, yet God has sustained and kept them. Don't let me keep you too long. We hear that the psalmist said something here, he said I've had the wrong concept, and I have had the wrong frame of mind, he said but that all changed when I went to church, he said all of that changed when I went into the sanctuary, he said that it all changed when I went into the house of the Lord.

Because in the sanctuary, here in the Tabernacle, is where God worked on me. Asaph said while I was at church my outlook changed, while I was in church my whole frame of mind changed, and some of you can testify, that there have been times when you came in one way, and while you were at the church God started working on you, and you didn't leave the way you came.

There have been times when you have come into the church frustrated over your situations, and God gave the preacher the right sermon just for you, or while you were sitting in your seat God may have given the choir the right song to sing to speak to your situations. Somebody ought to say it's in the church.

Now someone might ask, what does the sanctuary have to do with all of this, well I'm glad that you ask. Because the psalmist said I found the answers that I needed while I was in the church, and the answer to the million-dollar question is. The prosperity of the wicked is only temporary and it won't last. The evilness of the wicked will one day has to stand before Jesus. What I love about the joy that Jesus gave me is that I can say that this joy that I have, the world didn't give it to me and the world can't take it away. So, saints don't think it robbery when the enemy seems like they are prospering, because it's only for a short while. But if you are in Jesus, it will last forever.

I remember one time my family and I went to the carnival, and they were all riding this specific ride, and they said to me come on and let's ride this ride. Now the ride looked good from the outside, but I heard people screaming and shouting on the inside. I thought they were laughing and joking and having a good time. So, I boarded the ride, which began to spin uncontrollably. Inside, I saw unsettling images like goats, and demons on the wall that felt like they were draining me of my spirit. I called out to the conductor to stop the ride. Initially, he dismissed my concerns with a laugh, but on the second call, he recognized something was wrong and he halted the ride. I was carried off, and someone said, "That looks like Pastor Spies."

The conductor then asked me why I had chosen to get on the ride. I explained that from a distance, it appeared manageable. This experience serves as a metaphor for life:

things might look appealing from afar, and situations may seem better for others at the moment. However, in the end, when we receive our eternal reward, we will see that the wicked have ceased from troubling, and the weary find rest. All of God's saints and angels will sit at His feet and be blessed. So, what are you saying Pastor? I'm saying that one of these old days, we will see God for who he is, and we will be able to say:

You are a great God and your character is Holy.

Your truth is absolute.

Your strength is unending.

Your discipline is fair, you are a great God.

The mountain of your knowledge has no peak.

The ocean of your love has no shores.

The fabric of your fidelity has no tears.

The rock of your word has no cracks.

Your patience surprises us.

Your beauty stuns us.

Your love stirs us.

Your provision is enough for our needs.

Your light is good enough for our paths.

And your grace is sufficient for our sins, for Lord you are the potter, and we are the clay.

When you feel like quitting, I dare you to hold on.

Chapter Four
They Left Me Sitting On The Step Of The Church
Acts 3:1-12

As I was scanning through the scriptural regions, I stopped in the province of Acts chapter 3, and I looked at the scenes that were there. I quickly began to move to chapter 4 because I said, I have preached this text before, as I was turning the pages of the Holy Script, God said no go back because I want to show you something that you missed last time, I want you to go back to chapter two.

As I was reading this portion of scripture, I really don't know how much time that had elapsed between the events of Acts chapter two, and the occurrences of Acts chapter three or the exact duration of time between the concluding events of Acts chapter two and the commencement of Acts chapter three is not explicitly stated in the text, leaving the specific time gap open to interpretation. During my examination of this portion of scripture, I found myself uncertain about the duration between the events described in Acts chapter two and those in Acts chapter three. I must admit that I don't know the exact time interval between the concluding events of chapter two, and the commencing of chapter three remains unclear. But I do know that in Acts chapter two, the Holy Ghost had fallen upon the church. In Acts chapter two, the Day of Pentecost had fully come. In Acts chapter two, the Disciples and others from across the earth had gathered together, when all of a sudden there came into the building a mighty rushing wind.

In Acts chapter two, there appeared unto them cloven tongues as of fire that fell upon each one of them. In Acts chapter two, they were all filled with the Holy Ghost. In Acts chapter two, they became loud in their spiritual response. In

Acts chapter two, they were falsely accused, falsely evaluated and looked upon by bystanders saying, "These men must be drunk with new wine. But also, in Acts chapter two, there was one who faded into the background. There was one who had denied knowing, and being with Jesus, and now he is filled with the Holy Ghost, and he is speaking out boldly in Acts chapter two.

In fact, He preaches a sermon, and in his sermon, he is telling them that these men are not drunk as you suppose. He goes on to preach about The Prophesy of the Old Testament by saying that in the last days God will pour out His Spirit upon all flesh. It is said that in Acts chapter two, after that sermon was preached, some three thousand souls were added to the church. Yes, all of this happens in Acts chapter two.

In Acts chapter two the multitude is gather-together rejoicing, shouting and praising God, but now in chapter three, the excitement has died down. In Acts chapter three, the crowd has dwindled away. In Acts chapter two, a large crowd was present. Three thousand converts were there for the cause of Christ. But now in Acts chapter three, we just see two men walking together, by the name of Peter and John.

It is important to recognize that among those in the crowd, there are individuals who are present merely for the excitement or out of curiosity due to the novelty of the situation. However, not everyone in the crowd will remain steadfast. Some may withdraw at the first sign of difficulty, while others may abandon their commitment in the face of adversity.

In Acts chapter three, there are only two men. Look at the change that has now taken place by way of the marketplace. Understand that Peter and John really didn't have a great friendship with each other in Acts chapter two, but now we see Peter and John are walking together. Before the events of Acts chapter two, both seemed to irritate each other. They were so different in their personalities that one seems to get on the nerves of the other. Some of you can relate to people getting on your nerves.

You see, Peter was a protester, but John believed in a peaceful means of working out one's problems. Peter believed that violence was the answer to any problem, but John believed that talking it out was the best way. So, they both irritated each other, but that was before the Holy Ghost fell. And now after the Holy Ghost fell in Acts chapter two, by the time we get to Acts chapter three, they are walking together, and that's my first point: the Holy Spirit has the ability to unite us. The Holy Spirit fosters cohesion and transforms individuals into a unified team. While Peter and

John previously operated independently, they are now collaborating effectively.

It is critical to recognize that church work is inherently a team effort. It is not the responsibility of a single individual; rather, it requires collective effort. Each of us plays a role, and teamwork is essential to achieving our shared goals. We must understand that no one person can accomplish everything alone; our combined efforts are what drive success in our mission for Christ.

Allow me to make an important point: if we are indeed filled with the Holy Spirit, then we will work together harmoniously. If we are filled with the Holy Spirit, we will exhibit love for one another, pray for one another, and extend blessings to each other. They once were walking separately; they were once divided, but now look at them now, shoulder to shoulder. Look at them now, walking side by side and that's what the Holy Ghost will do.

So, now they are in the marketplace, and they had to get to the temple because it was now the hour of prayer. In route to the temple, before they could get to the temple, they had to go through by way of the marketplace. I think that we need to stop here and look at the marketplace.

First, I need to tell you what the marketplace is all about. There were merchants in the marketplace. There were salesmen in the marketplace. There were peddlers selling their wares in the marketplace. Also, there were thieves in the marketplace. There were women of the evening strolling in the marketplace, and Peter and John were on their way to the temple, but they had to journey through the marketplace. But may I tell you something before we leave the marketplace? I need to tell somebody that you can also find souls to save in the marketplace, so, please don't take the marketplace for granted.

Some individuals may adopt a superior attitude when navigating through the marketplace the need to emphasizing their titles of who they are such as Evangelist, Pastors, or Missionaries. This behavior often leads to reluctance to engage with others or interactions within the marketplace. However, it is essential to recognize that the church's mission extends beyond the confines of its walls.

Our true purpose and responsibility lie in actively engaging and serving in the broader community. If it hadn't been for the Lord's guidance, I would have been stuck in the marketplace. In my state, many people just walked past me there. I mentioned earlier that I struggled with chemical imbalances.

People were fine with that as long as I was on that organ during the eleven o'clock service. They didn't care about my struggles or sinful life, just as long as I fulfilled my role in the service. It made me feel like quitting. So many times, we pass the mission of the church on our way to church. Yes, we do church work, but not the work of the church. We walk with our choir robes in our arms, and we pass people who need to hear a good song in the marketplace. Sometimes with our Sunday school books and Bibles under our arms, we pass those who need to hear a Bible lesson in the marketplace. We want to preach and teach to each other. We want to fellowship with people who already know Christ and by-pass our mission which is in the marketplace.

Peter and John, after the Holy Ghost had fallen can now be seen making their way through the marketplace on their way to the temple. And on their way into the temple, they pass the gate of the temple, which was called Beautiful, and there at the gate was a victim of an unfortunate circumstance, here was a man, who was sitting at the gate. As Peter and John were entering the temple, there was a man seated there, holding a cup and soliciting alms from those who were entering the temple.

Now Peter and John had come at the ninth hour on their way to the temple and they found this man sitting at the side of the gate, what a tragic thing it was. Look at him with his cup rattling asking for handouts because he was lame and couldn't walk. The record is he was lame from his mother's womb. Because of his condition He couldn't work so He was forced to live on handouts of those who entered into the temple. I think I ought to tell you that it's sad, not that this man was born with an impediment. It's not sad because he was begging, but what's sad is that he is sitting in front of a crippled church.

He's at the temple, not in the temple. Maybe y'all are

not reading this. He was not in the temple; he was at the temple. That was the worst part of his problem. It was not how he was, but where he was. He was at the temple but not in the temple. He was brought there daily and laid at the gate. Now Peter and John walked up to him on their way into the temple. And the Bible says that the man lifted his cup and asked them for a donation. The record is Peter and John looked upon him, and the Bible said that Peter fastened his eyes upon him and said unto him, look on us, it is recorded that the man who was lame looked to them expecting to receive some money from them.

I can hear Peter saying, I know what you are expecting. I know what you are looking for. Down through the years, people have been dropping silver and gold in your cup, but yet your condition remains the same. Down through the years, people have been dropping money in your cup, but your circumstances are still in the same condition. Sir, silver and gold have not done you much good. You're still lame and you're still unable to move yourself from one place to the other, but yet you keep on asking for something that has not done you any good. You are doing the same thing and expecting different results. So, they said, in essence to him, we know what you've been asking for, but we need to tell you, that silver and gold have we none.

However, we want to offer you something that can truly make a difference in your life. The Bible describes how Peter extended his right hand to the lame man and helped him up. This act of lifting someone up is the fundamental responsibility of every child of God. As they reached out their hand, the lame man grabbed it, and immediately, strength was restored to his ankles. He stood up on his own two feet, and this shows us the working power of what God can do. He's able to stand you up on your two feet.

What the text is teaching us is that there is a danger in being at church, but not in church, because when you are at church and not in church, you miss the benefits that God has for you in the church. The Bible recounts that the man entered the temple, leaping and praising God, prompting some to question, "Isn't this the man who used to sit at the gate begging?" Instead of celebrating his healing and joining in his joy, they were preoccupied with questioning his identity and distinctiveness. They were more in a state of observation than they were in participation. However, this highlights how God has the power to transform lives visibly and profoundly, even in the presence of those who have passed us by.

Experiencing such moments of doubt and skepticism can make you feel as though giving up is the only option.

When others question your progress or the authenticity of your transformation, it can be disheartening and make perseverance seem incredibly challenging. These are the kind of things that make you feel like quitting. Many days, I felt as though I was left sitting on the steps of the church, despite being the presiding pastor. It reminds me of one was a crisp autumn morning when I first sensed the weight of my solitude. The church, a grand old building with its ivy-clad walls and stained-glass windows that stood majestically against the clear skies.

Yet, as I sat on the steps, I felt an unshakable sense of isolation. I had dedicated years to this congregation, preaching and guiding, yet lately, the sense of disconnection has grown. Members of the church were polite but distant, and the once lively community seemed to have lost its warmth. My sermons, filled with hope and encouragement, seemed to echo holy within the walls, reaching only a fraction of those who used to fill the pews.

One Sunday, after delivering what I thought was one of my most heartfelt sermons, I found myself alone on the steps once more. The congregation had trickled out, absorbed in their own conversations and lives, leaving me with my thoughts and the quiet rustle of falling leaves. As I sat there, contemplating my role and the impact I had on my flock, a young woman approached; she was a newcomer to the church. She had been attending for only a few weeks but had already shown a spark of genuine enthusiasm. "Pastor," she said with a warm smile, "I've been meaning to talk to you. I know you might feel alone sometimes, but your words have made a difference in my life. I've found strength and community here that I didn't expect." Her words, simple yet sincere, were like a balm to my weary spirit. We talked for a while, and I listened to her stories and dreams. In that moment, I realized that while I might have felt isolated, there were still connections being formed and lives being touched.

As we parted ways, her gratitude and optimism gave me a renewed sense of purpose. I knew that the journey wasn't always going to be easy, and there would be days when I felt alone on the steps. But those moments of connection, however small, reminded me of the impact I could have and the importance of continuing my work with dedication and hope, is when I knew that I Just Wanted To Quit, but the Lord said you Can't.

Chapter Five

I Can Call God When I Need Him

Jeremiah 33:1-3
¹Moreover, the word of the Lord came unto Jeremiah the second time, while he was yet shut up in the court of the prison, saying, ² Thus saith the Lord the maker thereof, the Lord that formed it, to establish it; the Lord is his name; ³ Call unto me, and I will answer thee, and shew thee great and mighty things, which thou knowest not.

While Jeremiah was imprisoned in the courtyard of the guard, the Bible recounts that the Word of the LORD came to him a second time. This signifies that God needed to reach out to him on two separate occasions to capture his attention. God delivers a message to Jeremiah instructing him to declare to Jerusalem that Babylon will advance from the north and devastate the city. This will occur unless the people repent, express remorse, and seek forgiveness.

Notice that King Zedekiah rejected the message and refused to repent. Often, when individuals dislike a message, they also harbor disdain for the messenger. In this case,

Zedekiah not only opposed the message but also took a personal affront to the messenger, Jeremiah. His dissatisfaction led him to imprison Jeremiah as a result of his anger.

Look at this, Jeremiah is locked up for doing the will of God. To me something just doesn't seem right about this situation. It seems like that if I'm obeying God, and doing the will of God, it seems like to me things are supposed to be perfect and flawless.

Unfortunately, the reality is quite different. The Lord Jesus instructed us that we are blessed when people revile us—meaning they insult, abuse, or condemn us—and persecute us, speaking all kinds of false evil against us for His name's sake. As I stated a few chapters earlier the Word of God is saying we are to "Rejoice and be exceedingly glad, for great is your reward in heaven."

The Bible teaches us that in times of insults, abuse, and false accusations, we should find reasons to rejoice. It's remarkable to think that God expects us to maintain our joy amidst such trials, with the promises of a significant reward awaiting us in heaven. Look at Jeremiah's issue. He obeyed God and people still mistreated him, insulted him, and locked him up.

So, while Jeremiah is going through, while Jeremiah is dealing with his storms, in the center of this dim, vague, blurred and unclear moment, Jeremiah is told to call on God. (Don't miss your shout again) This tells me that when we are going through, when we are having some hard times and difficult situations, that we need to call on the Lord. May I tell you that we can contact him when we are in trouble. We can call on him when we're in pain. We can turn to him in times of abuse.

We can seek for him when we're lost and unsure of where to go, and when we've exhausted all our options, simply call on him.

Let me call a witness to the stand. When King David was going through, he called on the Lord. Psalms 4:1-3 says, David made a request to the Lord in Psalm 4:1, He said *"Hear me when I call, O God of my righteousness: thou hast enlarged me when I was in distress; have mercy upon me and hear my prayer."*

Also, we need to remember to call upon the Lord when we are in trouble. Jeremiah was told, that if he called upon God, God would reveal to him great and unsearchable things. Allow me to convey that the same God who assured Jeremiah of revealing profound and inscrutable truths is the same God who will disclose these truths to us as well.

We may be wondering how we should call God. We

can call the Lord by bowing down on our bending knees. Ephesian 3:14 says *"For this cause I bow my knees unto the Father of our Lord Jesus Christ. We can call him on our bending knees."*

How can I call on him? Well, we should sing unto him, praise him and worship him. In 1st Chronicles 16:8-12 he says *"make known among the nations what He has done. Sing to Him, sing praise to Him; tell of all His wonderful acts. Glory in His holy name; let the hearts of those who seek the LORD rejoice. Look to the LORD and His strength; seek His face always. Remember the wonders He has done, His miracles, and the judgments He pronounced."* We must understand that God will respond when we seek Him in our distress. However, it is important to recognize that His responses may not always align with our expectations or be immediate. There will be instances when we must exercise patience, but rest assured, His timing is always perfect.

David's message is to reflect on God's past faithfulness. By doing so, while awaiting His response, we will maintain hope, avoid impatience, and remain steadfast. The Lord says, "Call to me," you don't have to depend on anyone else. Call me, I will show up. Call me, when others fail, I will never fail. Call me, and I will answer you and tell you great and unsearchable things you do not know.

Look what happened as a result of Jeremiah calling on God, God tells Jeremiah some of those great and unsearchable things. God tells Jeremiah exactly what He intends to do for Israel. God gives Jeremiah some precise, detailed, and some specific promises for the people. God says Jeremiah: I'll bring Judah and Israel back from their captivity.

God says Jeremiah: I will cleanse them and forgive them for their sins.

God says Jeremiah: your name will be a name of joy, and praise before others.

God says Jeremiah: there will be the sounds of joy and a voice of gladness.

God says Jeremiah: that day I will raise up my righteous branch who is Jesus.

And if he did it for Jeremiah, I must tell you again that he will do it for us.

The Lord God shared with this man of God (Jeremiah) promises after promises. He shares these promises with him in fragments to give him confidence and assurance that everything will be all right. From the text, I understand that perseverance through adverse circumstances is crucial. If we remain steadfast and resist the urge to abandon our efforts to lose patience, we can be confident that the Lord will provide for us. By holding firmly to His promises and seeking His guidance during times of trouble, and by recalling the assurance found in Romans 8:28—*"And we know that all things work together for good to those who love God, to those who are called according to His purpose"*—we can trust that everything will ultimately work out for our benefit. Just call on the Lord.

I know that I can call on the Lord, because the songwriter Sister Albertina Walker reminds me that I can go to God in prayer.

Verse 1 says makes no difference what the problem,

(I can go to God in prayer).

Yes, I have this blessed assurance,

(I can go to God in prayer).

He will take my gloom and sorrow,

(turn them into light).

He will comfort, strengthen and keep me,

(I can go to God in prayer)

I can call Him, when I need Him,

Our, Father, up in heaven;

I can go to God in prayer,

I can go to God in prayer.

But I really love Verse 2

Sometimes my burdens get so heavy,

(I can go to God in prayer).

I have found one who is so faithful,

(I can go to God in prayer).

I can call him when I need him our father up in heaven.

The Bible is filled with men and women who did the impossible because they kept their eyes on God, not on their circumstances. They called upon God and God delivered them in spite of the overwhelming odds that they faced.

Remember Moses led Israel out of Egypt with only a staff in his hand. David killed a giant with nothing more than a sling shot and a rock. Gideon and 300 men attacked and put to flight 135,000 Midianite soldiers with trumpets and torches (Judges 7:8).

Why did they succeed? Why were they able to overcome the overwhelming odds and difficulties? It was because they called upon God, and they relied upon His promises and his past faithfulness. That's the kind of God I serve. He's the kind of God that supplies all of my needs in His time and in His way, but always in a powerful and a wondrous way.

Someone may say well Pastor what is his number that I can call? Here are a few numbers that you call:

When in sorrow call John 14

When men fail you call Psalm 27

If you want to be fruitful call John 15

When you have sinned call Psalm 51

When you worry call Matthew 6:19-34

When you are in danger call Psalm 91

I'm reminded of a little story about a young Christian man by the name of Roy, who had died, and he goes to heaven. As he enters heaven gates He is met by St. Peter, who takes him on a tour of heaven. As they are going by this one beautiful golden building, he asked St. Peter what was in there. St. Peter said come and see. St. Peter opens the door to one of the rooms, and there are thousands of beautiful golden boxes with beautiful ribbons wrapped on them.

Roy looked at the boxes and he asked St. Peter What are those? St. Peter said, "These are blessings that God had up here for you, while you were down there on earth." Roy was a little upset and he was a little disturbed, he asked St.

Peter, why are they still here? Why did I not receive them?" he asked. St. Peter looked at him sadly and said, "because you never asked for them."

As a Christian he forgot that he could ask, and he shall receive. He forgot that we could seek and find. As a Christian he forgot to knock, and the doors will be open. Here it is, most of as Christians forget about Jeremiah 33:3, when I was ready to quit, I drop the ball on verse 3 which said Call unto me, and I will answer thee, and shew thee great and mighty things, which thou knowest not.

Chapter Six
I Must Decrease
St. John 3:22-31

When studying the Gospel of John, which I consider
to be the pinnacle among the four Gospels. Its profound
depiction of Christology is unparalleled, establishing it as
one of the most significant books in the New Testament. The
Gospel of John clearly establishes that Jesus transcends the
roles of Messiah, Son of Man, and prophet. It presents Him
as the embodiment of an invincible divine principle,
illustrating that He is the Word made flesh. In the first
chapter of St. John, the text meticulously articulates the
divinity of Christ, affirming that He is indeed God—the
same God who created everything from nothing,
commanding existence into being. As the scripture states, *"In
the beginning was the Word, and the Word was with God,
and the Word was God."* It further explains that all things

were made through Him, and without Him, nothing was made that has been made. In Him was life, and that life was the light of men, with the light shining in the darkness, which did not comprehend it.

The Gospel of John asserts the divinity of Jesus with such profound clarity and authority that it offers a portrayal of Christ that surpasses the depictions found in Matthew, Mark, and Luke. While the other Gospels provide accounts of His earthly actions, John presents a divine perspective, revealing Jesus' true nature and significance from a heavenly vantage point that extends back to the foundation of the world.

The Gospel of John provides details that are not mentioned in the other Gospels. For instance, in the account of Jesus raising Lazarus from the dead, John offers a specific and comprehensive information, whereas the other Gospels are either obscure, ambiguous, or vague regarding this event.

John's Gospel provides a profound insight into the encounter between Jesus and the Samaritan woman at the well. Unlike other accounts, John describes how the woman, who initially seeks water, encounters Jesus and finds a deeper fulfillment for her soul. This interaction is particularly significant given that the woman has had relationships with six men—symbolizing human imperfection—and then meets Jesus, the seventh man, symbolizing completeness and spiritual fulfillment. Jesus satisfies her deepest needs and prepares her for a new beginning, represented by the number eight.

For those seeking transformative experiences, it is essential to recognize the significance of a genuine encounter with Jesus. Ladies, it is important to value yourselves and establish clear boundaries in relationships.

Make it clear that any meaningful connection requires respect and commitment. Similarly, men should avoid superficial relationships, and both parties should seek authentic and respectful interactions rather than pursuing fleeting or transactional encounters.

It was the Gospel of John that provided us with the foundational scripture cherished by Christians, Protestants, and believers alike. This verse, which has been a cornerstone of our faith since we first began to grasp the teachings of the Bible, states: *"For God so loved the world that He gave His only begotten Son, that whoever believes in Him shall not perish but shall have everlasting life."* John 3:16.

Many of us have clung to this profound scripture, which has sustained and uplifted us through the years. We extend our gratitude to John for delivering such a powerful and enduring message. Indeed, this scripture remains as impactful today as it was over 2,000 years ago, from the moment Christ's blood was shed on Calvary. It is intriguing to note that while we often focus intensely on the initial sections of this chapter, we sometimes overlook the significance of its concluding passages.

This brings me to an important point about John. He was the leading preacher of his time, drawing crowds from far and wide to hear his message of repentance, proclaiming that the Kingdom of God was at hand. John possessed a remarkable ability to captivate audiences, his voice resonating even from the wilderness to the towns. Additionally, John was known for his unconventional and extraordinary nature.

Here's a nugget, people are drawn to those who stand out, and John certainly did. His diet of wild locusts and honey, along with his distinctive attire of camel hair garments, set him apart. His ministry was experiencing remarkable growth as a result.

To all of the Pastors, preachers, and those of you that are exploding, I think I need to tell you that you need to be careful who you let ride your coat tail while you're exploding, and moving fourth, because everybody that's riding with you is not for you. There are those that's on your bandwagon but do not care about you. Let me see if I can put it in hood term. You have some haters on your team.

Are you familiar with the concept of a hater? Haters are not individuals who dislike you for your possessions; rather, they are those who resent you simply because you achieved success before, they did. However, you should be grateful for your haters because they serve a purpose as catalysts for your advancement. According to the Bible, God will make your enemies your footstool, and a footstool job is to elevate you to heights you might not otherwise reach. Therefore, if you find yourself without any haters, consider seeking them out. You might even humorously offer them an application for their role, acknowledging their contribution to your rise.

John was at the Jordan River, performing baptisms while dressed in his camel hair garments, and bearing the aroma of wild locusts and honey. Despite his distinctive appearance, large crowds gathered to hear his message. When John saw Jesus in the crowd, the moment was profoundly transformative. He proclaimed, "Behold the Lamb of God, who takes away the sins of the world."

Given more time, I would further discuss the profound significance of this "Lamb of God." John was the first to identify Jesus as the fulfillment of the sacrificial lamb foreshadowed in Genesis. Just as Adam's nakedness was covered by the skins of a sacrificed animal, Jesus represents the ultimate realization of that sacrificial symbol in the New Testament. Today, Jesus remains my spiritual covering, and in times of adversity, I can steadfastly declare, "Behold the Lamb of God."

During times of trials and tribulations, I find solace in proclaiming, "Behold the Lamb of God." When facing difficulties in life or contemplating giving up, I can reaffirm, "Behold the Lamb of God." For every believer present, when the adversary seeks to undermine you by suggesting that he has a hold over you, stand firm and declare, "Behold the Lamb of God." Someone ought to affirm that in your spirit, "I am covered from the crown of my head to the soles of my feet, because behold the Lamb of God."

When I'm going through my trials and tribulation, I can stop and say behold the Lamb of God, when I'm having a difficult time in life I can stop and say behold the Lamb of God. When quitting is an option on the table I can stop and say behold the Lamb of God.

It is important to understand the dynamics of this situation: John's disciples are now disappointed because his following is dwindling. The once crowded balcony is now empty, only a few choir members remain in the choir loft, the once packed parking lot is nearly vacant, and the ushers have a surplus of programs. The church's fans are unused as congregants shifts their attendance to Jesus' ministry.

I can envision one of John's disciples approaching him, noting that Jesus' ministry is now attracting many of John's former followers. Rather than becoming disheartened or attempting to diminish Jesus' ministry, John responds with humility, acknowledging, *"He must increase, but I must decrease."* I must step aside to make way for Him."

One of the most challenging realizations we must come to is that our focus should not be on ourselves, but on Jesus. For instance, some individuals might brag about their long tenure in roles such as leading Sunday School for 30 years, questioning why growth is lacking. It could be because they are unwilling to step aside and allow for new leadership. Similarly, if a choir's performance suffers despite years of direction, it may be due to the leader's reluctance to embrace the guidance of the Holy Spirit. Some individuals may stubbornly cling to their positions, insisting that only their removal will prompt change. However, if necessary, God will ensure that such individuals are moved aside in a manner that ultimately aligns with His will.

Allow me to provide some context before concluding. Elizabeth and Mary were first cousins, with Elizabeth having conceived by her husband, Zechariah. According to the account, Elizabeth experienced no fetal movement for six months and had isolated herself from others during this time. While others were celebrating and discussing the miraculous nature of her pregnancy, Elizabeth maintained a quiet demeanor. She endured six months without feeling any activity from the baby. Then, six months into her pregnancy, Mary, her cousin, who was conceived by the Holy Spirit, visited Elizabeth while carrying Jesus.

When Mary arrived at Elizabeth's home and knocked on the door, Elizabeth welcomed her in. As Mary greeted her cousin, the moment their pregnancies connected, John began to leap within Elizabeth's womb. This reaction was not due to the conversation between Elizabeth and Mary, but rather the interaction occurring between Jesus and John in their respective wombs. I believe there are some individuals who are spiritually "pregnant" but experiencing a lack of growth or movement. They need a spiritually attuned "cousin" to visit and invigorate their inner spiritual state, awakening what remains dormant within their spiritual womb. What I find particularly noteworthy about this concept of spiritual pregnancy is that it applies to individuals of any gender. Both males and females can be "pregnant" with purpose, destiny, fulfillment, and hope.

The Bible tells that when the two mothers' bellies came into contact, the unborn babies began to leap within them. Some theologians may question where in the text does it specifically states that the mothers' bellies touched but consider the implications of two women who, are six months pregnant, coming into close proximity such as an embrace and their stomach does not touch. It is natural to infer that such an encounter would elicit a profound response from the unborn children.

John, the first recorded instance of someone being filled with the Holy Spirit while still in the womb, reacted with a significant movement upon encountering Jesus through Mary's presence. Elizabeth recognized this profound event, noting that something extraordinary had occurred. Similarly, encountering Jesus has the power to invigorate and transform situations that seem lifeless. If you are facing challenges that appear stagnant or dead, I encourage you to entrust them to Jesus, who possesses the power of resurrection.

Someone that is reading this need to know that something transformative is about to occur in their life, and that which once seemed lifeless is on the verge of revival. John, filled with the Holy Spirit, and Elizabeth, also filled with the Holy Spirit, are both significant figures in this narrative. Despite John never having seen Jesus, John sensed

His presence. For thirty years, John had not physically encountered Jesus, yet he remained committed to representing Him.

Imagine John proclaiming, *"Repent, for the Kingdom of Heaven is at hand,"* and declaring, *"I am not the Messiah, but one is coming after me whose sandals I am not worthy to bear."* John understood that he was not the one to usher in the new era; he recognized that someone greater was coming after him. While baptizing in the Jordan River, John adhered to his duties, saying, "In obedience to the great Head of the Church, we now baptize you," and proceeding to baptize individuals. Then, suddenly, he looked up and proclaimed, *"Behold the Lamb of God, who takes away the sins of the world."*

I can hear John acknowledging the need to step aside, recognizing that while he can baptize with water, Jesus has the power to baptize with the Holy Spirit. John understood the importance of making way for Jesus so that his divine work could be accomplished fully and that He might reveal Himself in all His glory. John knew he needed to step aside to allow Jesus to reach and transform the lives of individuals—whether husbands, wives, or children because his redemptive work could not proceed with John in the way. It is noteworthy that their initial meeting took place in the wombs of their mothers, and now, at their second encounter, they are in the waters of the Jordan River.

There is significance in this continuity of fluids. John's baptism of Jesus symbolized death, burial, and resurrection. When Jesus emerged from the water and the heavens opened, a voice from heaven declared, *"This is my beloved Son, in whom I am well pleased."* This underscores the necessity for us to step aside, as Jesus is now prominently present and active.

I can imagine John saying since Jesus is now on the scene blind eyes are being opened, since he's on the scene death ears are being open, since he's on the scene the lame is now walking, since he's on the scene cancer is being dried up, since he's on the scene my prayers are answered, since he's on the scene the dead is being raised, so we need to get out of the way.

When we get out of the way we will be able to say eyes have not seen, and ears have not heard of the great things that God has in store for us. When we get out of the way we will be able to sing bless it assurance because Jesus is mine. When we get out of the way we will be able to sing this little light of mine, I'm going to let it shine. When we get out of the way we will be able to sing amazing grace how sweet thou sound. When we get out of the way we will see people's lives changed. When we get out of the way the comforter will come. When we get out of the way, others will be able to lift their hands in praise. If you are trying to praise God and someone is obstructing your path, kindly ask them to step aside, because I can't give up now, and I can't give in now. The Lord has brought me too far to quit now. It's been hard but the Lord brought me through.

At this critical juncture, quitting is not an option. The progress made and the obstacles overcome thus far serve as a testament to the dedication and resilience invested in this journey. To abandon the effort now would not only undermine the achievements but also negate the sacrifices made along the way. The challenges faced have been steppingstones to growth, and persistence is essential to realizing the ultimate goal. Embracing the commitment to persevere, even in the face of adversity, ensures that the vision and purpose driving this endeavor will be fulfilled.

Thus, continuing forward with unwavering determination is imperative to achieving success and completing the mission that God has assigned to my hands.

Chapter 7

Excuses Excused

Exodus 3:10-15, 4: 1-17

In this Christian Walk of life, I noticed that we give excuses after excuses when it comes to the walk of life as a Christian and the service of God in the church. The excuses that we customize for God, would get us fired anywhere else. I have often considered how effective the church would be if we were to offer the same level of dedication, determination and devotion to the church as we do to other amusements, and pleasures. It just seems like we offer God more excuses than we do services. We give excuses of why we don't like church and why we don't go to church. I don't like the preacher; well, we are not there for the preacher. There are too many liars in there for me, they are at Walmart to, but you haven't stopped going there.

Some use the excuse that too many hypocrites are there, well, show me a church that doesn't have any. They hold service too long for me, you don't complain about overtime at the game. The music is too loud, no one ever tells the DJ at the club to turn down. It's too many sinners in there for me, but I've got some news for you this morning, and that is the only way that you can live above sin is if you live on the second floor and there is a sinner that lives on the first floor. Because the bible says that all have sinned and came short.

There are just too many excuses for why we don't, and not enough excuses for why we should. As we examine the lesson in Exodus 3, God tells Moses, Moses I have heard the cry of Israel for deliverance, liberation, and freedom, and he shares with Moses, Moses I am ready to deliver them. And then in verse ten we see the marching orders of God when God said, *"Come now, therefore, and I will send you to Pharaoh that you may bring my people, the children of Israel, out of Egypt."*

In this chapter what we will see is that when God confronts Moses with what he has for him to do, Moses then begins to complain and offer his excuses. And if we are honest and authentic, it seems as though some of us might be a relative of Moses, because some of us can see Moses within our own lives. Because God has mandated us to do some things and then the excuses start:

You're asked to teach a class – there is an excuse.

You're asked to minister to the youth – there is an excuse.

When you are asked to pray for others oh my spirit isn't right, I'm too busy, that's not my ministry. Often our excuses get in the way of doing the things God mandated us to do.

As we follow Moses, and the account of his life, Moses had a series of reasons for not wanting to hear the call of God. And as soon as God gave him the orders, Moses begins with a series of reasons as to why he should not be the right person for the job for which God had given him to do. He begins his excuses in chapter 3:11-12, when the Lord called him, his respond is who am I. Moses said to God, *"Who am I that I should go to Pharaoh, and that I should bring the children of Israel out of Egypt?"* Who am I, that I should go. Who am I that makes me qualified to go to Pharaoh?

I think that I need to tell somebody, to stop the who me syndrome. Because if God calls you, then God will qualify you, because this is the same God who knew you even before you were formed in your mother's womb. Moses said who am I? Moses should've known that the reason that God called him is because God knew who he was. One of the reason Moses probably found issues with this calling is that Moses probably recalled his earlier encounters of failures.

If you remember Stephen narrates and reports the events of what happen in chapter seven of the Book of Acts, (vv. 23-29), which says *"Now when he was forty years old, it came into his heart to visit his brethren, the children of Israel. And seeing one of them suffer wrong, he defended and avenged him who was oppressed and struck down the Egyptian. For he supposed that his brethren would have understood that God would deliver them by his hand, but they did not understand. And the next day he appeared to two of them as they were fighting, and tried to reconcile them, saying, 'Men, you are brethren; why do you wrong one another? But he who did his neighbor wrong pushed him away, saying, who made you a ruler and a judge over us?*

Do you want to kill me as you did the Egyptian yesterday?"
Some of you all know people have a way of recalling what
you did, but they always forget what they have done.

When Moses remembered that he had tried this
deliverance thing 40 years earlier, he remembered that he
was neither believed nor listened to, and he used this as one
of his excuses that if they did not listen to me 40 years prior,
why should they listen and believe me now? But what Moses
had failed to realize is that the people of Israel and he
himself are at a different spiritual place than they were 40
years earlier.

Things have shifted in the last 40 years. Some of you
can attest and confirm that things are not the same with you
as they were 40 years ago, because some of us didn't have
gray hair 40 years ago, and now some of us don't have hair

at all. Some people didn't have cell phones 40 years ago, but these days everyone has a cell phone. For some of us 40 years ago, we didn't know the Lord but look at us now. Moses was thinking about how things used to be, and he didn't realize that he was not the same as he used to be.

Moses was terrified of being rejected and feeling like a failure, but God comforted Moses in verse twelve; He said Moses you don't have to worry and be uneasy about the situation because "certainly I will be with you, and this shall be a sign to you that I have sent you: When you have brought the people out of Egypt, you shall serve God on this mountain."

Allow me to stop and encourage somebody with these promises, and that is, if the Lord sends you, you must know that he will be with you. If the Lord sends you then he will provide, protect and guide you. When we look at this story,

Moses excuses expressed the doubt within himself, and what we must learn is that God will never send us to do a job that we can't do. Secondly, "God says low I am with you always even until the end of the earth," which means that he won't send you out all by yourself. Moses primary excuse expressed doubts within himself, but in his next excuse Moses expressed doubt in God.

In verses 13-15 he wanted to know by what name am I going in, it's right here in the text. Verse 13 says, *"Then Moses said to God, Indeed, when I come to the children of Israel and say to them, 'The God of your fathers has sent me to you,' and if they ask me, 'What is His name, what shall I say to them?"* Yes, he doubted God. First of all, God didn't ask Moses to go and explain to the children of Israel, he just told him to go and when God speaks to us, we must understand that if God sends us, we don't need to understand why, we just need to be obedience.

But God responded to him in verses fourteen and fifteen, God said to Moses, tell them *"I AM WHO I AM."* And He said, *"Thus you shall say to the children of Israel, 'I AM has sent me to you." (15) 'The Lord God of your*

fathers, the God of Abraham, the God of Isaac, and the God of Jacob, has sent me to you. This is My name forever. God says, "I AM who I AM." What God was telling Moses, is that this doesn't have anything to do with who you are, but it has to do with who I am.

Now I kind of understand why so many people are not committed to God, it is because they don't know that God is sending them. They sort of know about Him. But like the Hebrews in Egypt some of us have lost track of who God is. That's why some are scared to witness for him. That's why some are scared to speak for him, and that's why some are scared to stand for him.

When God tells Moses that "I Am who I Am" he is literally saying that "I am He who was, and is, and always shall be. In other words, I will continue to be what I have always been. And that's God and God alone. Tell them that I am sent you. Look at his next excuse. *"Then Moses answered and said, "But suppose they will not believe me or listen to my voice; suppose they say, 'The LORD has not appeared to you."*

Moses' third excuse was, but suppose they will not? What if they ask me a question that I don't have an answer to?" I'm not an expert on the Bible, they might ask me a question that I do not know the answer to. Saints we must know that they (But suppose they will not), are victory killers, (But suppose they will not), are zeal quenchers, (But suppose they will not), are dream killers, (But suppose they will not) will drown your visions. But suppose they refuse to hear me?

You see Moses was so concerned about what might happen; that he didn't hear what God said would happen. God gave Moses supporting verifications that he was with him: First, his Staff turns to a serpent and back again (vv. 2-4). *"So, the LORD said to him, "What is that in your hand? He said, "A rod." (3) And He said, "Cast it on the ground." So, he cast it on the ground, and it became a serpent; and Moses ran from it. (4) Then the LORD said to Moses, "Reach out your hand and take it by the tail" (and he reached out his hand and caught it, and it became a rod in his hand), (5) "that they may believe that the LORD God of their fathers, the God of Abraham, the God of Isaac, and the God of Jacob, has appeared to you."*

It is important to note that God did not ask Moses to use something that he did not have. God asks Moses, what's in your hand? God uses what we have and will never demand from us to use what we do not have. We will never know the full potential of what can be done, until we are willing to offer what we do have. For God is not looking for ability, he is looking for availability. God's command to Moses is simple, "Throw it down." Okay that's simple enough, and he throws it down. Because of his obedience it becomes a serpent. And now the LORD says, *"Pick it up."* God says, Moses obeyed, and the snake again became a rod, and his faith is strengthened. So, we must know that in the act of obedience God will strengthen you.

Next, Moses is given the signs of his hand being made leprous then clean again (vv. 6-7) and the ability to turn water into blood (vv. 8-9). God has thus far revealed himself to Moses, and he told Moses of his desire to deliver the people, God promised him success, and given him three signs that the people will believe him. However, despite all this revelation God gave him, it's still not enough for Moses to believe. Because then Moses gives the Lord another excuse why he wouldn't be a good candidate for the job – he said, *"But Lord I Don't Speak Well"* (4:10-12) *Moses said to the LORD, Lord, I am not of eloquent speech, and I am slow of speech and slow of tongue."*

So, the LORD said to him, *"Who has made man's mouth? Or who makes the mute, the deaf, the seeing, or the blind? Have not I, the LORD? (12) Now therefore, go, and I will be with your mouth and teach you what you shall say."* Brothers and sisters, our inadequacies are not a problem for God, because he made us just the way we are. And if we do not make ourselves available then God's plan for our lives cannot go forward. So, I'm here to tell somebody don't worry about how well you talk, walk, don't worry about your education or your training, the Lord will give you what to say. Moses was worried because he studder, Moses was worried about his capabilities, but God was concerned about is availabilities.

With everything that God had given Moses he still had one more excuse, Moses said Lord just send someone else in verse 13 *"He said, O my Lord, please send by the hand of whomever else you may send."* And by this time the bible said that the anger of the Lord was kindle. I think that I need to warn somebody, that the last thing we want to do is make God angry. You might want to make your friends angry, but don't make God angry, you might want to make your family angry, but please don't make God angry. You see the problem was Moses didn't want to go.

This last complaint, this last protest, and this last opposition Moses gave was Lord, I just don't want to do it. Moses is simply putting his foot down and telling God, I don't want to do it. Exodus 4:14 says *"Then the LORD'S anger burned against Moses."*

Someone needs to make a note of this. God will become angry at our excuses when he knows the outcome of the case. And when he's angry His blessings are withdrawn. Moses was refusing to trust God's answer. When Moses ask God to send someone else, he is actually telling the Lord, "I don't trust you." And this angers God. In other words, what I am saying is, we do not need to send someone else to do what God is calling us to do.

So, as God is now angered, and finally in Exodus 4:20 we see a breakthrough in Moses. Moses finally knows that he is out of excuses, and he responds in an act of obedience. In Exodus 4:20: says *"So Moses took his wife and sons and put them on a donkey and started back to Egypt. He took the staff of God in his hand."* Moses finally did as the Lord asked him too and look at how many lives were saved because of his obedience. Look at the millions of Israelites that were delivered from slavery because Moses obeyed.

My brothers and sisters, when we walk in the obedience of God, we will touch the lives of those that are around us. When we walk in obedience, we can help others to be set free. Let me leave you with this final thought, on this journey. First, we must know that God is sending us. On this journey we must know, what God has put in our hands. On this journey we must know that God won't send us by yourself. And finally, on this journey, we must know that God will give us the victory.

We must know that everything that we need to work with, God has it for you. Don't allow any devil in hell to stop you from going fourth. If God tells you to sing, just sing and don't allow anyone to stop you because God has a reward for you. If God tells you to pray for the sick, preach the Gospel, teach the Word, or to Evangelize to the world, I encourage you to go fourth because God has a reward for you. Stop giving God excuses and start giving him service because all of your excuses have been excused.

I'm reminded of a story of a man whose lawnmower that was broken. He went next door to borrow his neighbor's lawnmower. As he knocked and knocked on the door, finally the neighbor came to the door and he asked his neighbor, neighbor may I please borrow your mower? The neighbor explained that he could not let him use the mower because all the flights had been canceled from Chicago to New York, and it doesn't look good tomorrow either. The borrower said wait a minute, you said all of the flights have been canceled from Chicago to New York and it doesn't look good for tomorrow either. It doesn't make sense, what does that have to do with me borrowing your lawnmower. The neighbor said it doesn't have anything to do with it, but I don't want to let you use my lawnmower and one excuse is as good as another."

We need to stop with the excuses and give God service because true devotion, requires more than just good intentions; it demands action. Excuses often mask our reluctance or lack of commitment, keeping us from fully engaging in acts of worship and service. By putting aside these rationalizations, we open ourselves to a more profound expression of faith, one that honors our beliefs through tangible efforts and genuine dedication.

Embracing service as a central part of our spiritual journey not only strengthens our relationship with the divine but also enriches our community and brings about meaningful change. It is through service that our faith is lived out, transforming abstract beliefs into concrete acts of love and compassion. This is why I remain committed to my path: every excuse I have presented to God regarding my limitations or reasons for hesitation has been met with the strength and resources He has provided me. Each challenge I face is countered by the tools and support I have received, reinforcing my resolve.

I recognize that the obstacles I encounter are not insurmountable, as I have been equipped to overcome them. This understanding empowers me to persist and continue moving forward in my journey. I can't Quit!

Chapter 8

Reasons Why We Can't Quit

Here are some compelling reasons why we should remain steadfast and not quit on our Christian journey:

1. **Divine Promise of Support**

   ➢ **God's Assurance:**

   The Bible assures us that God is always with us. In Matthew 28:20, Jesus promises, "I am with you always, even to the end of the age." This divine presence provides comfort and strength, reinforcing that we are not alone in our journey.

2. **Purpose and Calling**

   ➢ **God's Plan:**

   Each Christian has a unique purpose and calling. Ephesians 2:10 tells us, "For we are His workmanship, created in Christ Jesus for good works, which God prepared beforehand."

Quitting means potentially missing out on

fulfilling the specific plans God has for us.

3. Growth Through Trials

➤ **Spiritual Maturity:**

Trials and challenges are opportunities for

growth. James 1:2-4 encourages us to consider

it pure joy when facing trials because they

produce perseverance, leading to spiritual

maturity.

4. Witness to Others

➤ **Testimony of Faith:**

Our perseverance can be a powerful testimony

to others. Philippians 1:14 says, "And most of

the brothers, having become confident in the

Lord by my imprisonment, are much more bold

to speak the word without fear." Our

steadfastness can inspire and encourage others

in their faith.

5. **Eternal Rewards**

> **Heavenly Reward:** The Christian journey

promises eternal rewards. In 2nd Timothy 4:7-8,

Paul speaks of finishing the race and receiving

the crown of righteousness, which the Lord will

award to all who have persevered. Our

commitment to this life is rewarded in the next.

6. **God's Faithfulness**

> **Unfailing Love:**

God's faithfulness is unwavering. 2nd Timothy

2:13 states, "If we are faithless, He remains

faithful." Trusting in His promises and character

gives us confidence to continue, knowing He

will remain faithful even when we struggle.

7. Impact on Future Generations

➢ Legacy of Faith:

Our journey and perseverance can impact future generations. Proverbs 22:6 instructs, "Train up a child in the way he should go; even when he is old, he will not depart from it." Our commitment sets an example for those who follow.

8. Fulfillment of Joy

➢ Joy in Obedience:

Following God's path brings true fulfillment and joy. John 15:10-11 emphasizes that keeping Christ's commands result in complete joy. Quitting robs us of the joy and peace that comes from living in alignment with God's will.

9. Strengthening of Community

> **Support and Encouragement:**

The Christian journey is not meant to be walked alone. Hebrews 10:24-25 encourages us to "consider how to stir up one another to love and good works, not neglecting to meet together." Our perseverance contributes to the strength and encouragement of the Christian community.

10. Victory Over Adversity

> **Overcoming Challenges:**

Revelation 12:11 declares, "They overcame him by the blood of the Lamb and by the word of their testimony." Our faith and perseverance help us overcome adversity and challenges, affirming the power of Christ's victory in our lives.

These reasons underscore the importance of remaining committed to our Christian journey, drawing strength from God's promises and trusting in the purpose and rewards that lie ahead So, even if you want to quit, know that you can't.

Afterword

There is no other phrase in the English language that accurately describes the feelings of every human being at some point in his/her life than that of the subject of this book, "I Just Want To Quit, But I Can't." From the classroom teachers to police officers, to military personnel, to athletes, to politicians, we have all been overcome with this emotion. But no one is conflicted by this emotion like the one who carries the gospel of Jesus Christ. We are under divine orders to do so.

In this literary work, Dr. J.W.T. Spies effectively presents pictures of the conflicting journey of the divinely called carriers of the message of the master. We are often conflicted with the ever-present struggles between the flesh and the spirit, in ways that other saints cannot ascertain. The voice of the Lord has to be heard, and the preacher/pastor is under orders to be that voice. Though it is difficult, Spies give us a fresh dose of inspiration as he reminds us that he who sent us is also with us.

Gospel proclaimers all have a common mandate, which was thrusted upon us by our savior himself in Acts 1:8, "…and ye shall be witnesses unto Me both in Jerusalem, and in all Judea and in Samaria, and unto the uttermost part of the earth." This encouraging word put forth by my friend and brother J.W.T. Spies, helps us remain focused. We can't quit…the cause is too great.

Pastor Dr. Danny R. Hollins, PhD
Grace Inspiration Church, Jackson, MS
Cedar Grove Baptist Church, Pocahantas, MS

Afterword

Nothing worthy of reading is ever produced in a vacuum. No meaningful work is ever created in isolation. It takes a lifetime of experiences and diverse perspectives to recognize that we all need support.

If you've reached a point in your life where choices, challenges, and consequences seem to have come full circle, this book is essential reading.

While growth often comes through trials, it's also possible to avoid unnecessary hardships. Dr. J.W.T. Spies has profoundly impacted my life and others through his story and positive outlook on how God has ordained our lives.

I believe this book will inspire you to pray, act, and walk in alignment with God's purpose as you move toward your divine destiny. My hope is that this book will provide divine guidance that draws you closer to God than ever before.

It is my humble prayer that, like me, you find yourself refreshed, encouraged, and empowered to move forward into the abundant blessings God has in store for you. I Just Want To Quit But I Can't is a must read!

Thank you, Rev. Dr. J.W.T. Spies, for being my friend, brother and colleague.

Rev. Dr. Jonathan T. Phillips, Jr.
Rev. Dr. Jonathan T. Phillips, Jr.
United Baptist Church, Pearl MS
Mt. Zion Baptist Church, Canton MS

Made in the USA
Columbia, SC
07 November 2024

45931976R00076